FINDING TRUE PEACE

by

Michael Youssef, Ph.D.

Finding True Peace

ISBN 978-0-578-78623-0

Table of Contents

Introduction
It's Your Decision

In these troubled times, you may be asking, "How can I be free from the guilt and shame of the past? How can I be free from fear and anxiety about the future? How can I find true peace?"

My friend, you *can* have peace. You *can* have joy. You *can* face your past, knowing you are forgiven. You *can* face the future with confidence, knowing that God has a beautiful plan for your life. The Lord Jesus Christ wants nothing from you, and He wants to give you everything—through a relationship with Him.

Let me tell you how I found true peace, joy, and

purpose through the Lord Jesus.

Though I was raised in a Christian home in Egypt, though my parents and my seven brothers and sisters were all faithful followers of Christ, I was a rebel against God. Again and again, I broke my mother's heart with my sinful acts and my rebellion.

When I was born, my mother named me Michael—"messenger of God"—signifying her hope that I would dedicate my life to serving God. For years, she prayed for me and wept anguished tears over my wayward life.

One day, when I was fifteen, she took me aside, placed her hand on my head, and prayed out loud, "Lord, I have always prayed that Michael would be my one child who would preach your message with all his heart. But if I've been wrong, if Michael continues to rebel against you, then I pray you take him now."

I was stunned. She had actually asked God to take my life if I refused to submit to Him! That was my first realization of how deeply I had hurt my mother through my rebellion against God. Though I didn't immediately change my ways, my mother's prayer haunted me. I couldn't understand how my mother could love me with all her heart, yet would rather see me dead than living in disobedience.

Some months later, as I was struggling with my math homework, I went to my brother Samir (who eventually became a high government official in the finance ministry) and I asked him to tutor me. He said, "I'll help you with your homework—*if* you go with me to an evangelistic meeting."

I was cornered. I didn't want to fail math, so I agreed to go with Samir. But I wasn't going with an open mind—I planned to mock everything the preacher said.

Samir and I went to the service and sat down. The evangelist stood and preached from the Old Testament book of Hosea, in which God talks about being patient with His wayward children. But one day, God says, His patience will come to an end. On that day, judgment will come upon those who have taken His patience for granted.

Though I wanted to mock this message, I couldn't. I knew God had been patient with me—but now He was calling me to repentance. If I didn't heed His call, I might never have another opportunity. So, on March 4, 1964, I responded to God's invitation. I gave my life to Jesus—and He transformed me and brought true peace into my restless life.

The night I made my decision for Christ, my mother suffered a health crisis and went to the hospital. I went home and wrote her a letter, telling her I had committed my life to Christ. She kept that letter under her pillow—tangible proof that God had answered her prayers. Whenever someone visited her hospital room, she would pull that letter out and give it to them to read. Then she would say, "Now, I can die in peace." When I found true peace, God brought peace into my mother's life as well.

Four months after I went forward in that evangelistic service, my mother passed out of this life and into the presence of God. I am so glad I didn't wait another day to answer God's call. I'm grateful she died knowing that God had answered her prayers.

What a change God has made in my life. Before my conversion, I enjoyed sin—and I was a slave to sin. But when I committed my life to Christ, He set me free from the power of sin. As Jesus told His followers, "If you hold to my teaching, you are really my disciples. Then you will know the truth, and the truth will set you free" (John 8:31-32).

Today, our culture tells us that we don't need Jesus Christ to find God. Self-appointed leaders and spiritual "guides" tell us there are many ways to find God—through Buddhism, Islam, Judaism, yoga, a cult, a philosophy, a mantra, or some other belief system or practice. Others tells us we don't even need God—we can find a God-substitute or "enlightenment" by becoming involved in humanism, environmentalism, or social justice causes.

False teachers have infiltrated many churches, telling God's people that there are many paths to God. Some preachers and teachers who claim to be Christian have abandoned the teachings of the Bible, replacing sound biblical teaching with empty platitudes such as "love wins." They attract huge followings, but they are entertaining their congregations to an eternal torment. Like the serpent in the Garden of Eden, they tempt us to wonder, "Did God really mean what He said in the Bible?"

We may be witnessing the denial of faith that Jesus spoke of when He said, "At that time many will turn away from the faith and will betray and hate each other, and many false prophets will appear and deceive many people" (Matthew 24:10-11). When Jesus returns, I want to be found among those who remain faithful to Him and to His good news, even to the point of death.

The world may tell us there are many ways to God—but the world is lying. In Isaiah 45:21, God Himself said, "And there is no God apart from me, a righteous God and a Savior; there is none but me." And in John 14:6, Jesus said, "I am the way and the truth and the life. No one comes to the Father except through me."

Does it matter which path you take in your search for God and true peace? If you are sincere in your beliefs, isn't that enough? No. If Jesus is truly the way, as He claims, then by taking some other path you are sure to arrive at the wrong destination. Your sincerity won't help you if you are sincerely wrong.

My friend, you have a decision to make. No one else can make it for you.

Let's talk.

1

The Universal Problem

What is the sum of two plus two?

"Four," you say?

What if I told you that two plus two equals five? Would you still insist that the answer is four?

If I choose to believe two plus two equals five, who are you to tell me I'm wrong? Some might say that two plus two equals three. Others might say that two plus two equals a hundred or a thousand.

You may be thinking: "Two plus two always equals four. It's not a matter of opinion. It's a matter of fact."

Well, you have *your* truth, but someone else may have a *different* truth. Two plus two equals four might be the right answer for you, but who is to say it's the right answer for everyone?

Don't all paths ultimately lead to the correct answer?

The real world is intolerant of mistaken beliefs.

You may choose to believe that one liquid is pretty much the same as another. But if you fill your car's fuel tank with prune juice instead of gasoline, you'll discover that the engine of your car is intolerant of prune juice. And if you fill your juice glass with gasoline and drink it down, you'll quickly discover that your body is intolerant of gasoline.

In order to navigate our way through this world, with all its risks and dangers, we need to make sure our beliefs are rooted in reality. All paths do *not* lead to the same destination. If we believe things that are not true, if we start traveling down the wrong path, we are likely to end up at a different destination than the one we were hoping for.

In the beginning

The opening chapters of Genesis explain the

sufferings and sorrows that have tormented the human race throughout history. In Genesis, we find the source of our fear of death and our lack of true peace. We learn why we are plagued by a nagging sense of shame, guilt, anxiety, and separation from God.

Genesis begins with the Creator bringing the universe into existence out of nothing. He placed a formless Planet Earth in an empty void and divided the land from the water and the earth from the sky. He brought forth a myriad of life-forms upon the world. In the midst of it all, He created a beautiful garden called Eden. There He placed the first man and the first woman—Adam and Eve.

God created Adam and Eve to enjoy an intimate relationship with Him. The first humans experienced daily fellowship with their Creator. They had complete freedom to enjoy all the delights of the garden—except one. God placed a single prohibition on their freedom: "You must not eat from the tree of the knowledge of good and evil, for when you eat of it you will surely die" (Genesis 2:17).

But while God prohibited them from eating of

that tree, He also gave them the gift of free will. Adam and Eve were free to obey God—and free to disobey.

At the end of Genesis 2, we find Adam and Eve living an idyllic existence in their garden paradise. But at the beginning of Genesis 3, we encounter the serpent—Satan, disguised as one of the animals of the garden. The serpent asks the woman, "Did God really say, 'You must not eat from any tree in the garden'?"

Eve replies, "We may eat fruit from the trees in the garden, but God did say, 'You must not eat fruit from the tree that is in the middle of the garden, and you must not touch it, or you will die.'"

The serpent says, "You will not surely die. For God knows that when you eat of it your eyes will be opened, and you will be like God, knowing good and evil."

In other words, Satan told Eve, "Surely, God could not have meant that you would literally die. He would never be so intolerant as to deny you the experience of tasting the fruit of that tree. He just told you that because He didn't want you to become as wise as He is."

What does that statement remind you of? To me, it sounds very much like the voices we hear today: "Surely, Jesus could not have meant He is the *only* way to God. He would never be so intolerant. Jesus only said that because He wanted many people to follow Him. He's *a* path to God, but surely there are many *other* paths which ultimately lead to God."

The serpent offered Eve the false "wisdom" of this world. Seduced by the serpent's "wisdom," she took the fruit, ate of it, then gave it to Adam. And once Adam and Eve had tasted the fruit, they realized that, just as God had warned, there were consequences for disobeying God.

Genesis 3:7-10 tells us, "Then the eyes of both of them were opened, and they realized they were naked; so they sewed fig leaves together and made coverings for themselves. Then the man and his wife heard the sound of the Lord God as he was walking in the garden in the cool of the day, and they hid from the Lord God among the trees of the garden. But the Lord God called to the man, 'Where are you?' He answered, 'I heard you in the garden, and I was afraid because I was naked; so I hid.'"

Until Adam and Eve disobeyed God's commandment, they enjoyed a trusting friendship with their Creator. They lived in a state of true peace. After they disobeyed, their relationship with Him was broken. For the first time in their lives, they felt fear, inner turmoil, and shame. They covered themselves and hid from God's sight.

The sin of Adam and Eve placed a barrier between humanity and God that exists to this day. You and I still live with the tragic aftermath of that fateful choice.

The key to our humanity

Genesis tells the story of your origin and mine. It discloses what God has done in the past, what He is doing in our lives today, and what He will do in the future. We can't understand where we're going unless we know where we've been.

In Genesis we learn we are the children of Adam and Eve. The shame and fear that sin brought to their lives have been passed down to us through our spiritual genetic code. We identify with Adam and Eve. We sin just as they sinned.

The shadow of sin placed a vast gulf between the first humans and their Creator. God exiled Adam and Eve from the garden and sent them into the hostile world beyond. They began their new lives in the harsh wilderness outside of paradise. They could see their lost garden home, but they could no longer live there.

As the first farmer, Adam grew bronzed and weathered battling the weeds and thorns that threatened his meager crops. Eve suffered pain in childbirth—another consequence of sin. The children born to Adam and Eve became sinful, rebellious adults. One of their sons murdered the other, bringing grief and sorrow into their lives. Years passed. Adam and Eve grew old and died.

The human race multiplied, and so did human sin. The gulf between humanity and God grew wider and wider. The descendants of Adam and Eve created a civilization that openly defied God's rule.

Many people treat the story of Adam and Eve as a quaint fable—yet this story contains the key to our humanity. It explains why we are the way we are. It explains both our brilliance and our folly, our splendid achievements and our horrifying crimes. The story has been told and retold countless times over the centuries, yet it is still relevant in the Internet Age today.

The story of Adam and Eve tells us that we were created in the image of God, created for fellowship with Him, created for greatness. But the sin of Adam and Eve broke that fellowship and toppled our race from its unfallen position. You and I were created for the Garden; but the sin of Adam exiled us to the wilderness. The disobedience of the first human beings produced in us a spiritual "genetic disorder." The sin nature of Adam and Eve has been inherited by every child of Adam's race.

Just as sin separated Adam and Eve from their Creator, our sin separates us from God. That separation is the source of our lack of contentment, our guilt, our meaninglessness, and our fear of death. That gulf between us and God is the reason for the terrible emptiness so many people feel. We try to fill that emptiness by pursuing pleasure, wealth, power, and fame—but none of these things can bring us true peace.

But God has bridged the gulf between Himself and us. He has made it possible for us to return (in a spiritual sense) to the Garden, the place of peace. Many people are surprised to discover that

God begins bridging that gulf almost immediately after the sin of Adam and Eve. In the Garden of Eden, God reveals His plan of salvation for the human race: He is going to send a Savior.

We see this in Genesis 3:15, where God says to the serpent, "And I will put enmity between you and the woman, and between your offspring and hers; he will crush your head, and you will strike his heel." The "offspring" of Eve, of course, is Jesus. In symbolic language, which Adam and Eve could not fully understand, God promised the coming of Jesus the Messiah. Satan would strike at Him, tempt Him in the wilderness, oppose Him through the corrupt religious leaders, and ultimately nail Him to a cross. Thus, Satan would strike the heel of Jesus.

But Jesus would rise again on the third day. The day Jesus walked forth from the tomb, He crushed the head of Satan and destroyed the power of death. God's prophecy in Genesis 3:15 was fulfilled in the New Testament.

The story of Adam and Eve is told at the beginning of the Bible for an important reason. This story enables us to make sense of who we are as human beings, and it enables us to understand how we fit into God's plan for human history. The entire Bible, from Genesis to Revelation, is a unified and systematic whole. The books of the Bible tower like a brilliantly designed, well-constructed skyscraper—and the entire edifice rests upon the foundation of the Adam and Eve narrative.

The Scriptures show us what God did in the past so that we can understand what He is doing in our lives today and what He is going to do in the future. The story of the human race has a beginning, a middle, and an end. It's a story "written" in time and space, in the actual events of history. Through this story, the Author of these events makes Himself personally known to us. The better we know Him, the better we understand ourselves.

Between the beginning and the end

The beginning of the story of humanity in Genesis mirrors the end of the story in Revelation. In Genesis, human beings live in an amazingly beautiful garden, experiencing perfect fellowship with their Creator. In Revelation, resurrected human beings live in a beautiful garden city that comes down from heaven, and they experience the fellowship with God they were intended to have from the beginning. The lost innocence in the Garden of Eden is bookended by the restored innocence at the end of time.

The opening chapters of Genesis depict the first wedding—the union between Adam and Eve. Genesis 2 tells us that God made a woman from a rib taken out of the man, and God brought her to Adam. And Adam said, "This is now bone of my bones and flesh of my flesh; she shall be called 'woman,' for she was taken out of man." And Genesis adds (verse 24), "For this reason a man will leave his father and mother and be united to his wife, and they will become one flesh."

In a striking parallel, the book of Revelation presents another marriage ceremony. It is the wedding of the Bridegroom (the Lord Jesus Christ) and His bride (the church, made up of believers from every century and every nation). The writer of Revelation describes a voice like rushing waters and the sound of thunder saying, "Let us rejoice and be glad and give him glory! For the wedding of the Lamb has come, and his bride has made herself ready." Then, he said that an angel told him, "Write: 'Blessed are those who are invited to the wedding supper of the Lamb!'" (Revelation 19:7,9).

The parallels between Genesis and Revelation continue: In Genesis, God gives human beings authority over His creation. In Revelation, God's people are given authority to reign over creation with Jesus. Genesis begins with humanity's creation in a place of peace and joy. Revelation ends with redeemed humanity's entrance into a place of even greater peace and joy.

Heaven is described throughout the Old and New Testaments as a place of true and lasting peace. The prophet Isaiah writes, "'The wolf and the lamb will feed together, and the lion will eat straw like the ox, but dust will be the serpent's food. They will neither harm nor destroy on all my holy mountain,' says the Lord" (Isaiah 65:25).

Clearly, something important happens between Genesis and Revelation, between the beginning and the end of the human story. Something mysterious takes place to make that mirror-perfect ending possible. The problem of sin is solved. All our guilt, restlessness, fear, and shame—the symptoms of our spiritual "genetic disorder"—are healed. The human condition is transformed and we find true peace at last.

What takes place between Genesis and Revelation to bring about such a transformation in our destiny?

The answer lies ahead.

2

The Oldest Lie

Who is a true authority on cancer—the cancer patient or the cancer surgeon?

The patient knows cancer in an experiential way. He knows the sensations, the symptoms, the suffering, the dread, and the anxiety.

But the surgeon knows cancer in a clinical way. He has studied the pathology of cancer, its diagnosis, causes, treatment, and prognosis. He has examined cancer cells under a microscope, identified tumors in x-rays and MRIs, and has surgically removed cancerous growths from human bodies.

Both the patient and surgeon know cancer well. But they know cancer differently. The knowledge of the patient and the knowledge of the surgeon are different kinds of knowledge. The experience of the patient and the experience of the surgeon are as different as night and day.

The patient is a sufferer. The surgeon is the true authority.

In the Garden of Eden, Satan (in the guise of a serpent) came to Eve with the Big Lie. He said she could become a true authority on good and evil. He told her, in effect, that if she would disobey God, she could become the spiritual equivalent of a surgeon, having a complete and authoritative knowledge of this spiritual "cancer" called sin.

Eve believed the Big Lie. In so doing, she entered into the experience of sin. She became *not* an authority on sin, but a *sufferer* of sin.

In the previous chapter we saw the serpent ask Eve, "Did God really say, 'You must not eat from any tree in the garden'?"

She replied, "We may eat fruit from the trees in the garden, but God did say, 'You must not eat fruit from the tree that is in the middle of the garden, *and you must not touch it*, or you will die.'" (Note the phrase I italicized.)

At that point, Satan knew that Eve was ready to believe the Big Lie. How did Satan know this? Because Eve twisted God's command. In Genesis 2:16-17, God told Adam, "You are free to eat from any tree in the garden; but you must not eat from the tree . . ." Eve added something to that command that God never said: ". . . and you must not touch it . . ."

Perhaps Eve had already begun to question God's command. Every tree in the garden was hers to enjoy except one—yet it seems that her attention was focused on that one forbidden tree. Perhaps Satan had watched the woman as she walked around the tree, studying it from every angle. Perhaps he saw the gleam of curiosity in her eyes. Eve was fascinated by the tree—and Satan knew her area of weakness and how best to attack her.

So Satan approached her with the Big Lie. He said, "You will not surely die. For God knows that when you eat of it your eyes will be opened, and you will be like God, knowing good and evil."

In other words, "If you eat of the tree, you will

become wise, an authority on good and evil. Your understanding will be as great as God's understanding." Satan promised her that she would have knowledge of good and evil—and Satan's promise was half-true. By disobeying God, she would indeed experience sin. Once she was infected by sin, she would suffer from it and would come to know the difference between good and evil—in the most horrible way imaginable.

But Satan also promised that this experiential knowledge of sin would make her like God, with a God-like understanding of good and evil. And that was a complete lie. Satan still offers us the same Big Lie today, and people continue to fall for it.

When Eve took the fruit and ate it, she instantly knew the difference between good and evil—because she had just committed an act of sin. She had crossed the line from obedience to disobedience, from innocence to evil.

Her next act was to offer the fruit to her husband. Why did she do this? She had already condemned herself. Why did she proceed to invite Adam to join her? Perhaps in her selfishness, she didn't want to be alone. Misery loves company, and so does sin. Eve, knowing she had fallen into sin, didn't want to be alone. So she offered the fruit to Adam and invited him to eat.

Adam ate—and at that moment, he knew good from evil. Having tasted evil of his own free will, he lost the good.

So Adam and Eve fell—and we fell with them. As a result, the entire human race has come to know sin and evil in an experiential way. None of us is an *authority* on sin, but we all *suffer* from it.

The oldest lie in the book

If you are a skeptic, you might say, "But I don't believe in magical fruit growing on magical trees, which magically gives people the knowledge of good and evil. That's just a fairy tale for primitive people and children." Again, I'm not going to tell you what to believe. It's not my job to defend the Bible. The Bible can speak for itself.

But I will say this: The Bible does not tell us that there was any "magic" in the fruit. There is nothing in the Genesis account to suggest that any specific properties of the fruit caused Eve to become aware of the difference between good and evil.

I believe it was *the act of disobedience itself* that opened her eyes to good and evil. By choosing to disobey God's command, she entered into the experience of sin. The moment she chose disobedience, a profound change took place within Eve: She ceased to believe in God as God.

The moment Eve made her choice, she stopped believing in Him as her all-wise Creator and Friend. Instead, she convinced herself that God was preventing her from experiencing the goodness of the tree and the God-like knowledge of good and evil. She doubted that God truly wanted the best for her. In fact, she believed Satan's suggestion that God had *lied* to her.

Does the Big Lie of Satan sound familiar to you? If you believe in God, you have probably experienced times of doubt and questioning, when you've wondered if God is really wise and perfect, if He really wants the best for you, if He really loves you. You may have even wondered if God is telling you the truth, or if God is really God.

Perhaps you've wondered if the commands of God are meant only to restrict you and ruin your enjoyment of life. Maybe God doesn't really understand you at all. Jesus said He is the way and the truth and the life, the only pathway to God the Father—but what if that's a lie? What if there are many paths to God? What if there is really no heaven, no hell, but we are simply reincarnated and we keep coming back and living a succession of lives depending on the karma we accumulate?

These suggestions ultimately come from one source: the serpent in the Garden, Satan himself. The lie of "many paths to God" suggests, "A God of love would always allow people to come to Him by any road they choose—through living a good life, or through the teachings of Buddha or Mohammed, or through meditation and reincarnation or even hallucinogenic drugs. I prefer to believe that everyone is going to heaven whether they believe in Jesus or not."

Some of the best-selling books of our age preach and teach the Big Lie. One best-selling author tells us:

I want to offer the possibility that Jesus was truly, as he proclaimed, a savior. Not *the* savior, not the one and only Son of God. Rather, Jesus embodied the highest level of enlightenment.

He spent his brief adult life describing it, teaching it, and passing it on to future generations.

Jesus intended to save the world by showing others the path to God-consciousness [italics in the original].[1]

Notice the sentence in italics. Not only does this author tell us that Jesus is merely a savior among many (and just one path among many paths to God). Ignoring Jesus' own claims in such verses as John 3:16 and John 14:6, this author actually preaches that Jesus came *not* to save the world from sin but to point the way to "God-consciousness." In other words, this author claims that Jesus' message was the same message Satan gave to Eve: "Your eyes will be opened, and you will be like God."

Has there ever been a bigger lie than *this* Big Lie? Has there ever been another lie that people were so eager to accept? The author who wrote those words has sold millions of books, appeared on countless TV shows, and has been praised by world leaders. So the Big Lie is very popular in our culture today.

Books with titles such as *The Third Jesus*, *A Return to Love*, *A Course in Miracles*, *The Power of Now*, *A New Earth*, and *The Secret* all proclaim the Big Lie that human beings can become like God, can enjoy limitless health, wealth, love, sex, and eternal youth. All of these books sell millions of copies, which shows that people still fall for the oldest lie in the book.

Isn't it amazing? The people who buy these books think they are hearing the newest, latest "truths." Yet it's all the same Big Lie that Satan used to entice Eve in the Garden: "You can have everything you want by following *your* way instead of God's way."

Temptation and protection

When we have intimate fellowship with God, He offers us His divine protection, just as He offered protection to Adam and Eve. You might say, "*What* protection did He give Adam and Eve? If God was protecting them, why did they believe Satan's lie?"

God offers His protection, but He does not take away our free will. Adam and Eve were protected in the Garden of Eden, so that even the serpent,

Satan in disguise, could not directly harm them. Satan would have leaped at the chance to attack them directly and destroy the human race. But God would not allow that. There was only one way Satan could harm the first human beings, and that was through their own free will. Satan had to seduce them into choosing disobedience against God.

That's still the way Satan attacks you and me. When we walk in fellowship with God, He protects us from Satan's power. This doesn't mean we cannot get cancer or be killed in a traffic accident. It means that Satan has no control over us—unless *we* give him that authority through our own free will.

Satan will always try to seduce us into rebelling against God's plan for our lives. Our enemy knows we willingly deceive ourselves in order to serve our selfish desires. So Satan says to us, "Did God really say . . . ?" And he makes God's commands seem foolish or impractical. Like Adam and Eve, we have the power to choose Satan's lie instead of God's truth. We are subject to temptation—but we don't have to yield to it.

We can't simply ignore temptation and hope

it will go away. The voice of Satan is subtle and insistent. Temptation always forces us to make a choice: Yield to temptation or reject it. There is no middle ground. If you try to ignore temptation, it will keep coming back, calling to you, planting doubt after doubt, trying to break down your defenses.

How do you defeat temptation? There is only one way: You must reject it, firmly and finally. You have to say, "No!" to temptation—then call upon God to help you seal your decision and stand by it. Remove yourself from temptation: Unplug the TV or computer. Flush the liquor or drugs. Shun the so-called "friends" who keep pulling you back into your old, self-destructive habits. Ask a wise and trusted friend to hold you accountable and help you stand firm.

Our tendency is to move temptation just out of arm's reach—but not completely out of view. We like to deceive ourselves. We like to pretend we are trying to obey God. We go through the motions of resisting temptation for a while, knowing all the while that we will eventually give in. Satan doesn't even have to work hard to deceive us. We are so good at deceiving ourselves that Satan simply has to ask, "Did God really say . . . ?" We'll gladly do the rest.

So don't "flirt" with temptation—*flee* it. If you give temptation any toehold in your life, it will destroy you. It will cast you out of the garden and into the wilderness, just as it did Adam and Eve.

Temptation is a threat—and an opportunity. When tempted, we have an opportunity to place ourselves under God's authority and experience His victory. We have a chance to succeed where Adam and Eve failed. A trial of temptation reminds us that while we are powerless against Satan, we are not alone. We are protected by God's power, and He can give us the victory over Satan's Big Lie.

The Big Lie was first told in the Garden of Eden. The Lie continues to be told and retold to this day. Satan even tempted Jesus with the Big Lie in the wilderness of Israel. After Jesus had fasted for forty days, Satan offered Him food, kingdoms, and power if Jesus would reject God's plan for His life. Jesus resisted the temptation of Satan in the same way that you and I can resist him: by rejecting the Big Lie and clinging to the truth of God's Word (see Matthew 4).

The still small voice

Adam and Eve were created with the freedom to choose God's way or the Big Lie. They chose the lie.

From the moment our original ancestors made that fateful decision, our own genetic code has been tainted by the moral and spiritual virus of a naked self-will, of wanting our own way, of rebelling against God's plan for our lives. Centuries have come and gone since the Fall and we are still living that lie.

Worship of the self has replaced worship of God. We refuse to believe there is only one way of salvation, only one way to the Father. We choose to believe that there are many paths to God. Why? Because if there are many paths to God instead of just one, then we can choose the path *we* want. We can live the way *we* want, and never be held accountable by God. We can choose a religion that appeals to our own pride and vanity.

The Big Lie of Satan is so appealing to human nature that we actually hear it offered from some church pulpits and religious TV programs. Many preachers, ambitious for wealth and fame and a mass audience, have watered down the Lord's claim to be the only way to the Father. It doesn't matter how large a following a preacher has or how many books he has sold—if he tells you there is any path to God other than Jesus Himself, he is selling the same Big Lie that seduced Adam and Eve.

The Big Lie of Satan destroyed humanity's fellowship with God in the Garden of Eden. It continues to destroy human lives to this day. But you don't have to be deceived by the Lie. You *can* know the truth, and God's truth *will* set you free.

Adam and Eve once lived within the safe and protective enclosure of the Garden, walking and talking with their Creator, enjoying fellowship with Him. That is the life God intended for us all—and He still wants you to experience that way of life today. He wants friendship and fellowship with you. He wants to listen to your thoughts and feelings, your wants and needs, your hopes and dreams. Most important, He is eager to talk to you and guide you—if you will listen.

You may ask, "How can I hear God's voice?" You simply take time to read His Word, the Bible, where God has revealed Himself to the human race. Take time to pray. Speak honestly and openly to Him, just as you would talk to any friend. Sit quietly and clear your mind of all the busy, noisy distractions of this world. Be still and receptive to the gentle whisper of God's Spirit.

There is a scene in the Old Testament in which the prophet Elijah went up on a mountaintop to hear the voice of God. As Elijah stood upon the mountain, a great wind whipped up, breaking the rocks in pieces, causing an avalanche. But the Lord was not in the wind. Next, a great earthquake shook the mountain to its foundation. But the Lord was not in the earthquake. After the earthquake came a blast of fire. But the Lord was not in the fire.

After the fire came a gentle whisper—a "still small voice." That gentle whisper, that still small voice, was the voice Elijah heard (see 1 Kings 19:11-13). It was the voice of God's own Spirit. It was the voice of true peace. It's the same voice you and I can hear if we take the time to quiet our thoughts—and *listen*.

3

The Three Gardens

Russell H. Conwell, the founder and first president of Temple University in Philadelphia, wrote a book called *Acres of Diamonds*. He opened the book with a story he heard from a guide he hired in Baghdad in 1870. Conwell had hired this man to lead him to such ancient sites as Persepolis, Nineveh, and Babylon. This is the story the guide told Conwell as they rode on camelback:

Many years ago, a Persian farmer named Ali Hafed owned a large and beautiful farm in India. The farm was known for its bountiful grain fields and orchards and its lush garden. Ali Hafed was a wealthy man who was very contented. One day, a visitor from the east spent a few days at Ali Hafed's farm, telling him about special stones, left over from the creation of the world, made of congealed sunlight. These stones were called diamonds, and a handful of diamonds would make a man wealthy beyond compare.

That night, Ali Hafed couldn't sleep. He lay awake all night thinking about diamonds. Early the next morning, Ali Hafed went to his houseguest, the visitor from the east, and said, "Tell me where I can find diamonds!"

The visitor told him to find a river running through white sands, between high mountains. The diamonds would be in those sands.

So Ali Hafed sold his farm and went away in search of diamonds. He searched across India and into Palestine and on into Europe until he came to the Atlantic Ocean. In his travels, he had spent all his money and reduced himself to rags and poverty. In despair, he cast himself into the ocean and drowned.

But the story doesn't end there. The man who had purchased Ali Hafed's farm continued to tend its bountiful grain fields and fruitful orchards and lush garden. One day, the man led his camel into the garden to drink from the stream that ran through it. As the camel drank, the man noticed a flash, as bright as sunlight, from the white sands of the stream. He reached into the water and pulled out a stone that reflected all the colors of the rainbow. He took the stone into his house and placed it on the mantel of his fireplace.

One day, a visitor from the east—the same visitor who had told Ali Hafed about diamonds—stopped by the farmhouse. The new owner welcomed the visitor. Upon entering, the visitor looked at the mantel and said, "A diamond! Has Ali Hafed returned?"

The farmer was shocked to learn that he had found a diamond in his own garden—the first of many diamonds that would be dredged from the garden.

The guide from Baghdad concluded his story by telling Russell Conwell that the diamond that came from Ali Hafed's garden was the first of many diamonds from the fabulously rich Golconda diamond fields. It was the source of the crown jewels of England and Russia. Had Ali Hafed remained at home, tending his own garden, he would have found all the riches he searched for in vain.[2]

Treasures of truth and true peace are hidden in the three great gardens of the Bible. We find these three gardens occurring at three crucial moments in the story of God's dealings with humanity—at the beginning, the middle, and the end.

The first is the Garden of Eden—that place of peace and protection where Adam and Eve received the gift of life and experienced intimate fellowship with God.

The second is the Garden of Gethsemane, which we will explore in a moment.

The third is the garden at the center of the New Jerusalem. In the book of Revelation, John describes a scene from his vision of heaven: "Then the angel showed me the river of the water of life, as clear as crystal, flowing from the throne of God and of the Lamb down the middle of the great street of the city. On each side of the river stood the tree of life, bearing twelve crops of fruit, yielding its fruit every month. And the leaves of the tree are for the healing of the nations. No longer will there be any curse. The throne of God and of the Lamb will be in the city, and his servants will serve him" (Revelation 22:1-3).

The fruit of the tree in the first garden—the Garden of Eden—inflicted the curse of death on the human race. The tree in the third garden—the tree of life beside the river of life—yields a continuous harvest of life-giving fruit. The leaves of the tree are for the healing of nations. And the curse of death that was inflicted in the first garden shall finally be lifted in the third garden.

Clearly, something must have happened between the first garden and the third garden to bring about such a dramatic transformation. Some event must have taken place between Genesis and Revelation to completely alter the fate of humanity and lift the curse of sin and death.

That event, of course, took place in the second garden—the garden at the center of the story of humanity. That second garden was the Garden of Gethsemane—the garden at the foot of the Mount of Olives, outside the walls of Jerusalem. There Jesus struggled in prayer the night before He was crucified.

In the first garden, human beings were tempted by Satan to eat the forbidden fruit. In the second garden, Jesus—whom Paul called "the last Adam" or "the second Adam" (see 1 Corinthians 15:45-49)—faced a far more intense temptation. The first Adam was merely commanded not to eat the fruit of one tree—but the last Adam, Jesus, was sent on a mission to die upon another "tree," the cross of Calvary.

In that second garden, the perfect Son of God was tempted to reject God's plan for the human race, to reject the agony of the cross, to reject total separation from God the Father. The temptation Jesus faced was so excruciating that prayer itself became agony, causing sweat to pour from His brow like drops of blood.

There in Gethsemane, Jesus battled Satan through absolute reliance on God the Father. He drew upon the same Source of strength that is available to you and me in times of temptation. In that garden, Jesus settled the matter, saying, "Not My will but Yours be done." He chose obedience, submitting Himself to the Father's will and surrendering His life on the cross. His obedient submission guaranteed the defeat of Satan. There, Jesus crushed the head of the serpent, fulfilling God's promise in Genesis 3:15.

In the first garden, Adam and Eve yielded

to Satan, ate the forbidden fruit, and by their disobedience infected all of their physical descendants with the virus of sin. In the second garden, Jesus drank the cup of judgment for us all and healed us of the deadly "sin virus." You can be healed if you respond to Jesus and receive the gift He offers you. The gift is free—but you must accept it. Once you receive the gift, you'll be raised to life by the One who defeated Satan and overcame death.

It's your choice. As long as you choose to live apart from Jesus, rejecting the true peace He offers, you will live in the shadow of guilt and fear. You will remain outside the garden, exiled in the wilderness.

What about hell?

If you accept the notion that all paths lead to God, then logically you must also believe that there are no paths that lead to hell. If all paths lead to God, then hell is either empty or does not exist. The problem with this view is that hell is spoken of repeatedly in the Scriptures. In fact, most of what we know about hell is revealed by Jesus Himself.

Jesus described hell as a literal place of eternal punishment (Mark 9:43-44; Matthew 10:28; 13:40-42; 18:8-10; 25:46; Luke 16:22-31). Hell was designed as a place for the punishment of Satan and the fallen angels (Matthew 25:41; Rev. 20:10), but it will also be a place of punishment for those who reject God's free gift of salvation (Revelation 20:12-15). You may choose to believe that all paths lead to God, but Jesus clearly warned against hell and He described it in graphic detail.

It breaks my heart to look around the Christian landscape and see that there are some churches that have stopped teaching the words of Jesus and now falsely claim that all paths lead to God. Some churches now ignore most of what Jesus actually said. They especially ignore His claim to be the only way to God the Father.

A minister once sat in my office, glaring at me in anger. "I don't understand how you can be so arrogant," he told me. "How can you say that Jesus is the only way to heaven?"

"I'm not the one who invented this idea," I replied. "Jesus Himself said, 'I am the way and the truth and the life. No one comes to the Father except through me.' You're a Christian minister, so I would think you would consider yourself bound to teach the words of Jesus Himself. Instead, you substitute your own human reasoning in place of what Jesus actually taught."

We had a long conversation. In the end, he clung to his rationalizations and I clung to the words of Jesus. He was not persuaded by my arguments nor by the Scripture passages I showed him.

So I ask you: Is it arrogant to teach that Jesus is the only way to heaven? I certainly don't feel superior to anyone when I preach that message. I don't feel superior to a Buddhist or a Muslim or an atheist. I feel humbled that God chose to show grace to a poor sinner like me.

But if I wanted to become popular in this world, I would not preach such a message. We who proclaim Jesus to be the only way to heaven are always in hot water. We who preach this message are called narrow-minded, bigoted, and intolerant. We are criticized for preaching a message that other faiths find offensive.

People have asked me, "How dare you say that a Buddhist or a Muslim or a sincere atheist cannot go to heaven, simply because he doesn't agree with your religious views?"

I reply, "No one will ever go to hell because they disagree with me. My opinions are of no importance. But I fear for those who reject the teachings of Jesus. I fear for those who reject the sacrifice of Jesus. I fear for those who reject the grace of God."

So if you are sitting in a church, and you hear the minister say that there is no such thing as a literal hell, or that the hell described in the Bible is merely a metaphor, then I suggest you leave that church as quickly as possible. That is a church which ignores the most central teachings of Jesus Himself. You will not find God's truth in that place.

You might ask, "How could a loving God send anyone to hell?" The answer might surprise you: God never sends anyone to hell. All who end up in hell, whether human beings or Satan and his demons, are there because they have placed themselves there by their own choice. They have refused to accept the grace of God.

What is grace? According to the Bible, grace is the goodness and mercy of God extended to undeserving, sinful human beings—to you and me. We don't deserve grace and we can't earn grace. We can only thank God for His forgiving grace to us.

At a great cost to Himself, our loving Father has made it possible for *everyone* to receive eternal life in heaven with Him. He sent His only Son to suffer and die on the cross so that we would not have to endure the punishment of hell. The New Testament tells us, "The Lord . . . is patient with you, not wanting anyone to perish, but everyone to come to repentance" (2 Peter 3:9). Clearly, God has no desire to send anyone to hell, but He will not overrule our own free will. If we choose an eternity in hell, He will not send us to heaven against our will.

You might ask, "But what about those who have never heard the good news about Jesus Christ?" People have asked me that question hundreds of times. Here is my answer: Don't worry about those who haven't heard. They are God's responsibility, not yours. What is your responsibility? Simply this: Once you have heard the Gospel of Jesus Christ, you must make a decision. What will your decision be? Will you accept the true peace that God offers you through His Son Jesus Christ—or will you reject His grace?

4

The Temporary Solution

Animal sacrifice—the ritual killing of an innocent animal—has been practiced in almost every culture and history, from the ancient Hebrews to the Greeks and Romans of ancient Europe to the Hindus of ancient Asia to the Mayans, Aztecs, and Incas of the ancient Americas. There seems to be an instinctive awareness in the human psyche that human sin demands a sacrifice.

In the first book of the Bible, we discover how that awareness came to be implanted within the human soul. In Genesis 3, after Adam and Eve introduced sin into the world, we read: "The

Lord God made garments of skin for Adam and his wife and clothed them" (Genesis 3:21). This was the first instance of animal sacrifice in the history of the human race. The significance of the garments of skin is twofold:

First, the animal skins covered the nakedness of Adam and Eve. After the first humans ate the forbidden fruit, Genesis 3:7 tells us, "Then the eyes of both of them were opened, and they realized they were naked; so they sewed fig leaves together and made coverings for themselves."

Before they sinned, nakedness had never been a cause for shame. But once Adam and Eve crossed over into disobedience and sin, they realized their nakedness. They could not hide their sin. They tried to hide it by covering their bodies with fig leaves sewn together, but their attempt to hide their sin was hopelessly inadequate. God had to provide a covering for the nakedness and shame of their sin—and our sin.

Second, the death of the innocent animal was a symbol. It pointed forward to the day when the innocent Lamb of God would be sacrificed upon a cross. The slaughter of the animal was a visual lesson to Adam and Eve of what God would have to do in order to save them and their descendants from the curse of sin.

The Bible doesn't tell us what kind of animal God killed to make garments of skin for Adam and Eve. I suspect that the slain animal was a lamb—the fleecy white symbol of gentleness and innocence. Throughout the Old and New Testaments, the lamb symbolizes Jesus as the sacrifice for our sins.

I also believe that God made Adam and Eve watch as He slaughtered the sacrifice of the innocent animal. It was the first time they had ever witnessed death. By killing the lamb before their horrified eyes, God set before them a symbol of what it would cost to rescue humanity from the deadly curse of disobedience.

That first sacrifice was a *picture* of the coming Deliverer, the promised Savior who would come in perfect innocence and be slain in full view of a watching humanity. But the sacrifice of the innocent lamb was only a *temporary* solution to the sin problem. It pointed ahead to the *perfect* and *permanent* sacrifice that would take place centuries later—the sacrifice of the Lamb of God upon a cross in Palestine.

Though the blood of an innocent animal is a startling symbol, an animal's blood is powerless to save anyone from sin. Only the blood of the sinless Son of God can rescue us and bring forgiveness, salvation, and true peace to Adam's race.

The tragedy of Cain

Adam and Eve understood that the death of the animal symbolized God's promise of a coming Deliverer. From that day forward, the entire human race looked forward to the coming of the Savior. In fact, when Eve gave birth to her first child, she named him Cain, a word which in Hebrew suggests "he is brought forth" or "he is here."

This name tells us that Eve mistakenly believed that Cain was the Savior whom God had promised, the Deliverer who would crush the serpent's head and erase the curse of sin. Eventually, it became clear to Adam and Eve that Cain was not the promised Deliverer. In fact, he grew to become a self-willed and rebellious young man.

Cain grew up outside of Eden, having never

known the paradise his parents had lost. He never experienced the close fellowship his parents once had with God. Adam and Eve tried to teach Cain right from wrong, but he was spiritually dull, and their teaching couldn't penetrate his self-centered will. He grew up to become even more disobedient than his parents.

The story of Cain is the story of the first murder. Cain planted crops, and his younger brother Abel was a shepherd. Adam and Eve taught their sons the importance of making sacrifices to the Lord. Cain brought a portion of his crops to God as a sacrifice, while Abel brought the firstborn sheep of his flock. God accepted Abel's sacrifice of firstborn lambs because they conformed to the sacrificial ritual He first showed Adam and Eve. Only the death of an innocent lamb could symbolize the death of the coming Messiah.

By offering grain from the soil as a sacrifice, Cain showed that he missed the point of the sacrifice. Perhaps if Cain's heart had been right with God, he would have known why his sacrifice was unacceptable to God. But Cain was rebellious and angry. God urged Cain to change his attitude and make his heart right before God.

"Why are you angry?" God said. "If you do what is right, will you not be accepted? But if you do not do what is right, sin is crouching at your door; it desires to have you, but you must master it."

Cain refused to listen to God's gracious pleadings. Instead, he lured his brother Abel into a field. There he attacked his brother and killed him.

When God came to Cain and asked him where Abel was, Cain lied. "I don't know," he said. "Am I my brother's keeper?" His reply dripped with resentment and sarcasm.

God asked, "What have you done? Listen! Your brother's blood cries out to me from the ground. Now you are under a curse and driven from the ground, which opened its mouth to receive your brother's blood from your hand. When you work the ground, it will no longer yield its crops for you. You will be a restless wanderer on the earth." God exiled Cain for murdering his brother, just as He exiled Cain's parents for their sin.

Centuries of prophecy fulfilled

Some people wonder why God punished Adam

and Eve so severely for violating a command which seems (from a human perspective) seemingly minor: "You must not eat from the tree of the knowledge of good and evil" (Genesis 2:17). Some would say, "Why was God so mean to Adam and Eve? All they did was pick some fruit off a tree and eat it. It's not as if they *killed* anybody."

But notice what a short distance it was from the sin of eating the forbidden fruit to the sin of murder. How Adam and Eve must have blamed themselves for willfully defying the Creator! From that one act of sin flowed more horror and suffering than they ever imagined possible: One son slain, the other exiled. And that was only the beginning of sorrows to come.

Adam and Eve had more children, and their children had children. Years went by. Generation after generation watched and waited for the coming Deliverer whom God had promised. The Old Testament sacrifices were vivid reminders that a Savior was coming. The human race suffered through century after century—the time of Noah, the time of Abraham, the time of Jacob, the time of Moses. God raised up prophets in

Israel, who recorded God's thoughts in the pages of the Old Testament.

Down through the ages, the prophecies of the coming Messiah became clearer, more detailed, more specific. The prophet Micah predicted His birth in the town of Bethlehem (Micah 5:2). The prophet Isaiah foretold His virgin birth (Isaiah 7:14), His role as the Prince of Peace (Isaiah 9:6), His anointing by the Holy Spirit (Isaiah 11:2), His message of good news (Isaiah 61:1), His miracles (Isaiah 35:5-6), and His rejection and death (Isaiah 53).

The prophet Zechariah predicted that He would enter Jerusalem as a king, riding on a donkey (Zechariah 9:9), and that He would be "pierced" (as by a spear or by the nails of the cross; Zechariah 12:10). The prophet Daniel predicted that he would be presented to Israel as king 173,880 days after the decree to rebuild the city of Jerusalem (Daniel 9:24-27)—a prediction that was fulfilled exactly to the day.

The Psalms predicted His rejection (Psalm 118:22) and the piercing of His hands and feet along with other specific details of His crucifixion (Psalm 22; 34:20; 69:21). The Psalms also predicted His resurrection (Psalm 16:10) and His ascension into heaven (Psalm 68:18; 110:1). And this list barely scratches the surface of the hundreds of Old Testament prophecies that clearly identified Jesus of Nazareth as the promised Messiah and Deliverer.

Finally, the long-awaited, long-predicted moment arrived, and the baby Jesus was born to a virgin in the little Judean town of Bethlehem. The baby grew to become a Man. And that Man fulfilled all of the Old Testament prophecies—including the very first Old Testament prophecy, Genesis 3:15, in which God told the serpent in the Garden of Eden, "He will crush your head, and you will strike his heel."

Satan struck the heel of Jesus at the cross of Calvary. But when Jesus died and rose again, He crushed the head of the serpent. He destroyed the curse of sin and brought us true peace with God. He set humanity free from the fear of death. He opened the gates of heaven, so that all who believe might go in.

Spiritual "gene therapy"

The apostle Paul reminds us that the genetic

disorder of sin is always at work in our human bodies. "What a wretched man I am!" he writes. "Who will rescue me from this body of death?" (Romans 7:24). We want to do good, yet the destructive effects of the sin disorder are constantly at work in our lives. Sin is not just something we *do*; it is a part of *who we are* as descendants of Adam and Eve. We are genetically predisposed to rebel against God.

Our God is a just God, and we stand guilty before Him. The court of heaven declares that if we violate God's laws (and we can't help but do so), then we will spend eternity separated from Him.

Many people find God's judgment difficult to accept. They refuse to acknowledge the awfulness of their own sin. "I'm a good person," they say. "Sure, I sin from time to time, but on the whole, I think my good deeds probably outweigh the bad. If I do enough good works, God will accept me."

But that kind of thinking is not rooted in reality. Moral justice is not a scale with our good works on one side and our sin on the other, and we hope the good outweighs the bad. We can never pay for our sins with good deeds. We can never make ourselves acceptable to God by our own efforts. We can't earn God's approval or work our way to heaven.

Good works are the essence of every other religion on earth. All other religions involve striving to earn God's favor, striving to achieve moral perfection. We see this in the Jewish ceremonial law, the eightfold path of Buddhism, the Hindu doctrine of *karma*, and the *sharia* law of Islam.

The essence of Christianity is not human effort, but God's grace. The concept of grace is unique to Christianity. It is not found in any other religious belief system. The doctrine of grace not only teaches that we don't *need* to earn our way to heaven; it teaches that it's *impossible* to earn our way to a heaven. The apostle Paul put it this way: "For it is by grace you have been saved, through faith—and this not from yourselves, it is the gift of God—not by works, so that no one can boast" (Ephesians 2:8-9).

So it's a fatal error to think, "I've lived a good life. I don't need to be saved." At the same time, it's also a fatal error to think, "I've lived such a sinful life that I can *never* be saved."

People have said to me, "Pastor Youssef, you have no idea how sinful I am. I have lived a wretched life. I'm a slave to sin. God cannot possibly forgive someone like me. I'm doomed to a life of guilt and shame—and I know that when I die, I'm destined for hell."

The truth is that God's grace is greater than any sin you have committed. Where did you get the idea that your ability to sin exceeds God's ability to forgive? Instead of focusing on yourself and your sin, think about God and His love for you. Instead of focusing on your past, think about the amazing future God wants to give you.

We cannot earn our way to heaven. We are all under the curse of Adam's sin, and we are all unworthy of salvation. No matter how far we have fallen, we cannot fall beyond the reach of God's love and grace. He has forgiven, redeemed, and restored sinners of every kind—blasphemers, murderers, robbers, slave-traders, adulterers, and worse. Nothing you have done comes as a surprise to God. He is ready to receive you—yes, even you!

Though we are genetically inclined to sin, God's grace is spiritual "gene therapy" that heals us and gives us God's power to overcome temptation and sin. God has given us the gift of His Son, the gift of true peace. All He requires of us is that we accept that gift through faith.

All-encompassing—and totally free

We were all born with a debt we can never repay through good works. In fact, the Bible tells us that the wages of sin is death (Romans 6:23). But God has made full payment for our debt and He has saved us from eternal death. In His love and grace, God sent His Son to die on a Roman cross and rescue us from our sin. Jesus, God's sacrifice of Himself on our behalf, died voluntarily. He died with a heart bursting full of love for you and me.

As the Bible tells us, "For God so loved the world that he gave his one and only Son, that whoever believes in him shall not perish but have eternal life" (John 3:16). The only one ever born without the weight of sin around His neck was Jesus. He was the only One qualified to take your place and mine, the only One who could pay our debt. Once we accept the gift of God's grace, three amazing things take place:

1. *God delivers us from the defeat of the past.* As children of Adam, we are born dead—spiritually dead. All our efforts to make ourselves acceptable to God are doomed to defeat. But the grace of God erases the sins of the past, delivers us from death, and turns defeat into victory. His grace heals the "dis-grace" of our genetic sin disorder and makes us not just children of Adam, but God's adopted heirs.

2. *God gives us a victorious life in the present.* As Paul tells us, "But because of his great love for us, God, who is rich in mercy, made us alive with Christ even when we were dead in transgressions—it is by grace you have been saved" (Ephesians 2:4-5). We were dead because of our genetic sin disorder, but God made us alive with Christ—truly a radical transformation! As a result of being alive with Him, the "sin genes" we inherited from Adam no longer control our daily lives.

Though we still sin, our desire is to serve God. Though we have trouble in this fallen world, we have true peace with God. He makes His power available to us, day by day and hour by hour. We can call upon Him to set us free at every moment, whenever we are tempted. The apostle Paul reminds us, "And God raised us up with Christ and seated us with him in the heavenly realms in Christ Jesus" (Ephesians 2:6). That is a present-moment promise, not a future promise. *At this very moment* we are connected to a heavenly power source that enables us to live as God intended.

We don't have to work up more faith. Even our faith is a gift from God. All we have to do is accept this gift and exercise the faith God gives us. We can't take credit for God's grace. All we can do is give thanks for His gifts.

3. *God gives us a thrilling future.* In fact, He gives us *two* futures.

First, God gives us a bright future in this life. He makes our daily lives meaningful and purposeful. We no longer merely exist, but we truly *live* to serve Him. The good works we do in service to Him will never be lost or wasted. As Paul tells us, "For we are God's workmanship, created in Christ Jesus to do good works, which God prepared in advance for us to do" (Ephesians 2:10).

Our good works do not save us, but they do give us a sense of purpose in our lives. As we serve Him, we have the thrill of knowing that we are ambassadors and servants of the King of all creation. The work we do for Him is infinitely and eternally important.

Second, God gives us a future in eternity with Him. Nothing we experience on earth can compare with the blessings God has planned for us in heaven with Him. It will be an unending future of adventure, joy, and pleasure in His presence. Our eternal future with Him is what we truly long for throughout our lives.

Think back to the most perfect day you've ever experienced: Hiking through the Grand Canyon . . . a day at Walt Disney World . . . witnessing a space shuttle launch . . . watching the most beautiful sunset imaginable . . . the moment of your wedding . . . the birth of your first child. Whatever that most perfect and thrilling moment of your life might be, an infinitely greater *eternity* awaits you in heaven with the Lord. Every joy of this passing life is just a foretaste of the endless joys that await us in God's presence.

Past, present, and future . . . this life and the life to come—the grace of God transforms everything. When we truly know Him, intimately and personally, everything is changed.

5

Beyond Our Understanding

One of the most powerful and emotion-laden words in the English language is "home." When you are home, you are warm, secure, and protected. You belong. You are loved. You have food to eat, a bed to sleep in, and a roof to keep out the rain. Those who value home the most are those who are farthest from home: A soldier overseas, a prisoner in a cell, a patient in a hospital bed, a runaway child in a strange city.

One of the best-known, best-loved stories in the Bible is the story of a runaway who wandered far from home. The story—the Parable of the Prodigal Son and the Loving Father—is told by

Jesus. Many people have heard of this so-called "Prodigal Son" without truly understanding what the word "prodigal" means. It's not a word we hear very often in any other context. To be prodigal is to be wasteful, wanton, and reckless with one's spending.

The story of the Prodigal Son is recorded in Luke 15:11-32. There, Jesus tells the story of a willful, selfish young man who goes to his father demanding his entire inheritance on the spot.

What is an inheritance? It is the property that is passed on to an heir after the owner of that property dies. So this son, in effect, says to his father, "I can't wait for you die. I want what is coming to me now. Whatever you're going to leave me in your will, give it to me right this minute!"

The son's words were shocking and scandalous to those who heard Jesus tell the story. It was as if this young man had gone to his father and said, "Drop dead!" The son *insulted* his father, revealing what an ungrateful, self-centered, and insensitive young man he was.

Yet the father loved his son so much that, instead of taking offense, he gave the young man what he demanded—a staggering sum of money. Cash in hand, the son turned his back on his father and walked away, intending never to return. Despite the young man's disrespect, the father's love was undiminished. He stood at the door and watched his son leave home. He waved, but the rebellious boy never looked back.

The depths of degradation

The young man wandered off into a distant land. He spent his money on good food, the best wine, and prostitutes. He shared his money with other people and made many so-called "friends." He gave no thought to the future, nor to what would happen after his money ran out.

When his pockets were empty, his so-called "friends" abandoned him. Penniless and friendless, he was completely alone in an alien land. He had no home to go to. He had wasted his inheritance.

Finally, he was forced to take a job feeding hogs. There was no job more humiliating for a Jewish man than feeding pigs—animals that were ritually unclean according to the Jewish faith. He was so hungry he resorted to eating the vile food meant for the pigs. He had sunk as low as he could go.

So the young man thought of home. He remembered his father. He had always sneered at his father's old-fashioned values, his preaching about hard work and thrift. But now all of his father's "old-fashioned" ideas made sense. The harsh reality of life in a hog pen caused him to see his father from a different perspective.

The young man realized that, had he not been so self-centered, he would still be in his father's house enjoying three square meals a day. If only he could go home—but he had no right to expect anything from his father now.

Then he had an idea. Perhaps he could return home and *beg* to be taken back—not as a son, but as a servant. Even if his father threw him out in the street, he'd be no worse off than in a hog pen.

So he started out for home. Along the way, he planned out a little speech: "Father, I have sinned against heaven and against you. I am no longer worthy to be called your son; make me like one of your hired men."

As the young man neared his home, his father saw him in the distance. This father must have gone out every day, watching for his son, hoping to see him, hoping to welcome him home. Jesus tells us that the father was filled with compassion for his son and "he ran to his son, threw his arms around him, and kissed him." In the original language of the New Testament, Jesus says that the father kissed his son eagerly and repeatedly.

Do you see how much this father loved his son? Imagine the hurt this young man had inflicted on his father—yet his father loved him with an overflowing love. In fact, the father shouted to his servants, "Quick! Bring the best robe and put it on him. Put a ring on his finger and sandals on his feet. Bring the fattened calf and kill it. Let's have a feast and celebrate! For this son of mine was dead and is alive again; he was lost and is found!"

The radical concept called "grace"

Most of us, as we listen to the Parable of the Prodigal Son and the Loving Father, identify with the son. We all know what it means to want our own way, to be headstrong and self-willed. And we know what it means to suffer the consequences of our sin. We are well-acquainted with the sting of regret.

Yet this story is not primarily about the son. It's about the father. It's a story about God's free gift of grace—the gift of His lavish goodness in our undeserving lives. This concept of grace, which is at the heart of the Christian faith, saws across the grain of every other religious faith on earth. The people who first heard Jesus tell this story were steeped in Jewish ceremonial law, which supposedly enabled people to *earn* God's favor through rituals and rites.

When Jesus told this story, he presented the father as a man of "amazing grace" who freely forgave his wayward son. The father never demanded an apology or an explanation. He never ordered the young man to make restitution or work off the debt. He never said, "I told you so," or, "I hope you've learned your lesson." No, the father received the son, kissed him repeatedly, and celebrated his return. That's how God the Father receives you and me.

This story unveiled the radical doctrine of God's grace. None of Jesus' hearers had ever heard such a thing before. The idea that human beings could simply return home to God and be forgiven— why, this was unthinkable! Yet, when Jesus told the people about this loving and gracious Father, a light broke through the clouds to illuminate their hearts.

Grace is a concept beyond human understanding. Only God in human flesh could have disclosed such a remarkable idea.

Grace makes no sense

Ask yourself: Why would the father receive the son back with open arms? The young man deserved nothing but rebuke and rejection. This ungrateful son had spurned his father's love and had never looked back.

Why did the young man return? Because he had experienced a change of heart? No. He had come back because he had nowhere else to go. He had run out of money. He had squandered everything his father gave him. He was hungry and destitute. The father didn't know that his son had genuinely repented. In fact, the son might have returned only to take advantage of him.

Logically, it was the height of foolishness to show grace and forgiveness to this young man. Grace made no sense to the first century Jews who first heard the story of the prodigal son. And the story makes no more sense today.

A suburbanite father in North America would have no more reason to take back a rebellious and morally dissipated son today than a first century father in the Middle East. Grace makes no sense— yet grace is the heart of the Christian gospel.

Why would God offer forgiveness as a free gift to people who willfully reject Him, rebel against Him, and insult Him? Why does God watch for us and pursue us and draw us to Himself? The nature of grace is rooted in the nature of God. We can only understand grace when we understand who God is.

Grace—not leniency

There are two types of grace described in the Bible.

Theologians call the first form of grace "common grace." I prefer to call it "mercy." Common grace or mercy is the undeserved goodness God freely gives to all human beings. Jesus spoke of this kind of grace when He said that God "causes his sun to rise on the evil and the good, and sends rain on the righteous and the unrighteous" (Matthew 5:45). Everyone is permitted to enjoy the goodness of

God's creation, whether they love Him or not.

The second form of grace is called "special grace." This is a grace God gives to all who accept the free gift of salvation through Jesus. This is the grace the loving father gave to the prodigal son. It's the grace you and I, as sinners, are invited to receive from our heavenly Father—the inexhaustible riches of God's goodness which He showers on us despite our sin.

If you have received Jesus as your Savior and Lord, and God has received you in His open, loving arms, then you have experienced "special grace" from God. It's the grace that calms our fears, erases our guilt, and gives meaning to our lives.

Many people mistake God's grace for permissiveness or leniency. They seem to think that God looks upon our sin with a kind of easy-going tolerance, saying, "Oh well, they sinned again, but it's not such a bad sin. People will be people, after all. I'll just look the other way and pretend not to notice."

If you think He simply lets our sins slide by unnoticed, you are making the same mistake Adam and Eve made in the Garden of Eden—

and the same mistake Cain made when he killed his brother in the field. They thought they could sin and God wouldn't notice.

Nothing escapes the notice of God. He does not wink at sin. When we sin, there is a price to pay. Grace is neither permissive nor lenient. Grace is neither free nor cheap. Grace is the costliest, most precious commodity in the universe. It cost God the infinitely precious lifeblood of His only Son.

There is only one basis on which you and I may receive God's grace: the death of Jesus Christ on the cross at Calvary. If Jesus had not obediently chosen to accept death in that moment of decision in the Garden of Gethsemane, there would be no grace for you and me. We would be dead in our sins.

The grace of God is His goodness toward us—goodness that is infinitely beyond what we deserve. Grace was made possible by the death and resurrection of Jesus Christ.

God's grace is inexhaustible. There is no depth of sin which God's grace cannot cover. But His grace will not go on forever. One day it will cease. When the grace of God comes to an end, judgment will take place.

Our God is an infinite and eternal God. He has no beginning and He has no end. But there will one day be an end to His grace. So, while His grace is still offered to us, freely and abundantly, let us accept it with gratitude. Let's revel in it and enjoy it and thank God for it—but let us never take it for granted or treat it as mere permissiveness or tolerance of sin.

The inexhaustible grace of God is the most exciting and exhilarating aspect of the Christian life. Receive it—and every facet of your life will be transformed.

The Parable of the Prodigal Son and the Loving Father tells us that when we wander away from our "home" with God, we bring suffering upon ourselves. When we live apart from Him, we waste our lives. All the things we think we want—money, excitement, sexual thrills, popularity—will eventually leave us lonely and destitute. Our foolish choices will leave us in the "hog pen" of despair.

God, our loving Father, receives lost and undeserving sinners. He loves us even though we have insulted Him. He loves us even though we have gone far away from Him and have wasted all of His blessings. God not only waits for us to return, but He watches for us. He intensely desires that we come to Him for salvation, reconciliation, and true peace.

Sin produces death

There are some important parallels between this story and the story of Adam and Eve. The prodigal son lived an ideal life while he was in his father's house. Everything the father owned was his to enjoy. Yet the son was not satisfied. He thought he needed to go far from home to find peace and fulfillment.

In the same way, Adam and Eve lived an ideal life in the Garden of Eden. Everything God had created was theirs to enjoy. Yet they were not satisfied. Tempted by the serpent, they thought they needed to taste the forbidden fruit to be happy and fulfilled.

The prodigal son sought fulfillment in forbidden pleasures; so did Adam and Eve. The prodigal son spurned the blessings he already possessed; so did Adam and Eve. The prodigal son elevated his own wants and reasoning above that of his father. Adam and Eve elevated their own wants and human reasoning above the commands of their Creator. Just as the prodigal son thought he knew better than his father, Adam and Eve thought they knew better than God Himself.

God told Adam and Eve not to eat of the fruit of the one tree—but Eve put the forbidden fruit to a test. Perhaps she wanted to know what its texture was like, or how it tasted, or what its nutritional value might be. Perhaps she thought, "I have experienced every fruit of this garden but one. I must experience this fruit, even though it is forbidden."

So she tasted it. The fruit seemed sweet at first, as so many forbidden experiences do. She decided the serpent was right. God was wrong. So she took the fruit to her husband and offered it to him.

The prodigal son also put the "forbidden fruit" to the test. He wanted to know what it was like to party all the time, to live his life as an endless riot of wine, women, and song. He wanted to experience every sensual pleasure, even if it was "forbidden fruit." So he took a big bite out of life and it tasted sweet at first. But it ultimately left him impoverished and destitute, eating food that reeked of the pig sty.

People still feel they haven't lived until they have tasted all the forbidden experiences life has to offer. They think, "If God were really good, He wouldn't deny me the things I want. If I obey His commandments, I'm going to miss out on something good. My life won't be complete. Since God's Word prohibits so many of my desires, God's Word must be wrong."

That's why so many people end up enslaved by addictions and sinful habits. They lose their reputations, their families, their careers, their self-respect. In the end, they may even lose their lives and their immortal souls. Truly, the wages of sin is death.

The moment Adam and Eve ate the fruit, they died—just as God warned they would. You might think, "No, they ate the fruit—and nothing happened!" But something *did* happen. After they ate, they hid themselves from God. They separated themselves from the intimate fellowship with God they had once enjoyed.

Why did they hide from God? Because they were spiritually dead.

Physical death would follow, but spiritual death

came instantly. Their friendship with God was replaced by fear—fear of punishment, fear of God's disapproval. That fear is one of the signs of spiritual death.

Why didn't Adam and Eve experience physical death as well as spiritual death at the moment they ate the forbidden fruit? Answer: God's grace. Their Creator allowed them to continue living, even after their spiritual death, so they would have an opportunity to repent and return to Him.

In His grace, God also promised them a Savior who would come into the world, crush the serpent's head, and save Adam's race from sin and death. At the time, Adam and Eve couldn't understand all that God was telling them. The promise of the coming Messiah was shrouded in mystery.

But at least they understood that God was not going to leave them dead in their sins. Centuries would pass before the angel Gabriel would appear to Joseph and Mary, announcing that a child would be born to them—a child conceived by the Holy Spirit. The angel told Joseph and Mary to name their child Jesus (in Hebrew, *Yehoshua*, meaning "God delivers"), because He would save

His people from their sins.

Many long centuries before the child was born to Joseph and Mary, another couple, Adam and Eve, watched as God slaughtered an innocent animal in front of them and made garments to cover their shame. In this way, Adam and Eve were made to understand that innocent blood had to be shed so that their sins could be forgiven. Through the sacrifice of that innocent animal, God taught Adam and Eve that an innocent must die for the sins of the guilty.

Though Adam and Eve did not fully understand that lesson, they caught a glimpse of the amazing truth that the sinless Son of God would one day die in their place. That glimpse was enough. From that day forward, Adam and Eve placed their faith in the One who would come and save His people from their sins.

Why did Jesus have to die?

Why did it have to be that way? Why did Jesus have to suffer and die on that cross? Why didn't God simply shout from heaven, "All is forgiven—I'll wipe away your sins and pretend they never happened"?

The reason we ask such questions is that we do not comprehend the awfulness of sin. We think, "I'm not a bad person. I didn't kill anybody. I didn't steal anything. I'm not an adulterer. I didn't commit any of the *big* sins. I'm not perfect—who is? But I haven't done anything that deserves death!"

If those are your thoughts, consider these facts: Adam didn't kill anybody. He didn't steal anything (who was there to steal from?). He didn't commit adultery (his wife was the only woman on the planet). He didn't commit any of the so-called "*big* sins." What was the sin that caused God to send Adam and his wife out of the Garden of Eden? Simply this: Adam chose his own way instead of God's way.

That was all Adam did—and it was enough for God to exile him from paradise. And remember, Adam did exactly what people still do today. We choose our own way instead of God's way.

Many people think that the belief that "all paths lead to God" is a new and enlightened concept, but it's the oldest lie in the world. It's the Big Lie that was first told in the Garden of Eden, and which continues to be retold in books and magazines and TV shows every day. It's the desire to please God *your* way, to be accepted by God *your* way, to think you can make it to heaven *your* way.

But there is only *one* way to God the Father. He opened that path to us through His Son, Jesus. "I am the way and the truth and the life," He tells us. "No one comes to the Father except through me" (John 14:6).

That is God's last word on the subject of our salvation and true peace. We can only come to God the Father through Jesus alone. There is no other way.

6

The Indescribable Gift

I once heard a story of a wise and benevolent king who loved his people and wanted to know how they lived. So he would dress in the clothing of a beggar and go out among his people. They didn't recognize him, so they spoke freely in his presence. He could ask them any question, and they would always answer candidly.

On one occasion, he visited the home of a poor man who lived in a tiny shack at the edge of the village. Though the man owned next to nothing, he invited the disguised king to come in by the fire and share the meager bread and wine he possessed. The bread was dry and the wine was sour, but the king sat at the man's table, ate, and talked. The poor man was kind and cheerful, and the king enjoyed the man's company.

A few days later, the king returned to the shack of the poor man—and this time he came in his royal robes, riding in a carriage. The poor man instantly recognized him as the visitor who had visited in disguise. "You are my king!"

"I am indeed," the king said. "I enjoyed our visit so much that I returned to offer you a gift. What would you like? Gold? A new house? The best food the kingdom has to offer? I love to give good gifts to my people."

"There's no need of that, my king. You've already given the greatest gift you could ever give me."

"I haven't given you anything."

"Oh, but you have! You came from your palace to visit me in my shack. You ate with me and talked to me. You made my heart glad. And now I know that the one who visited me was the ruler of the kingdom. You have given me the gift of yourself. I want nothing more than that."

At the first Christmas, the King of creation left His home in heaven and walked among us, giving us many gifts. Born of a pure virgin, living a perfect and sinless life, He healed the sick, raised the dead, and preached the forgiveness of sin—yet He was crucified on a criminal's cross. God gave Jesus to the human race as a Christmas gift. That is the true meaning of Christmas.

We tend to lose sight of this profound truth during the scurry and rush of Christmastime. We become focused on planning family gatherings and buying gifts. We put a lot of thought and care into the gifts we buy for family and friends. Yet these gifts all have one factor in common: They are all describable. Whether the gift is a toy for a child or clothing for an adult, it can be described and explained.

But the gift God gave to the human race is indescribable . . .

Inexplicable . . .

Unfathomable . . .

Why? Because the gift God gave at the first Christmas was fully God and fully man, and completely beyond human understanding. Jesus was a divine gift, a supernatural gift—a gift possessing a quality I call "the God factor." That is why Paul, in 2 Corinthians 9:15, writes, "Thanks be to God for his indescribable gift!"

The natural and the supernatural

Jesus is the only Christmas gift worthy of the name. If you receive the gift of Jesus, you will be richer than the richest billionaire, happier and healthier than any earthly ruler, safer and more secure than the strongest army on earth. This may sound like an exaggeration, but it is the literal truth. Jesus, God's Christmas gift to us, is an indescribable gift.

For 2,000 years, the world's greatest minds have tried to describe the indescribable gift—without success. Great artists have tried to depict God's gift with paint on canvas or chiseled stone. Great musicians have tried to describe God's gift through such works as Handel's *Messiah* or Bach's *Jesu, Joy of Man's Desiring*—yet as beautiful as these works are, they fall short of describing the indescribable gift. Not even the angelic choir in the sky above the shepherds' field, announcing the birth of Christ, could do justice to the gift. It is simply indescribable.

The seventeenth century English poet Richard Crashaw expressed a deep truth in these lines from "A Hymn of the Nativity":

Welcome all wonders in one sight,
  Eternity shut in a span,
Summer in winter, day in night,
  Heaven in earth, and God in man,
Great little one, whose all-embracing birth
Lifts earth to heaven, stoops heaven to earth.[3]

What a profound expression of the true nature of God's gift at the first Christmas. Yet even these words are inadequate to fully describe the Christmas gift God gave to us.

God's indescribable gift is unique because it is supernatural. How can you explain the fact that our God is one God in three Persons—the Holy Trinity—Father, Son, and Holy Spirit? Who can fathom the astounding truth that our Creator-God became a man?

That which is natural can be described and explained. But that which is supernatural is beyond description.

No middle ground

The impact of this gift on our lives—like the gift itself—is indescribable. The pure and sinless God carried the sin of the whole world—your sin, my sin—on His sinless body. How can we explain the fact that the immortal God dies? How can we explain the fact that He and He alone can rescue us from eternal damnation and take us into heaven?

The self-existent God who has no beginning and no end—the infinite, eternal, unchangeable God—has entered into our world, has taken on our humanity, has become a human being like us, but without sin. How can we explain the fact that He and He alone is Emmanuel—God with us?

The indescribable nature of Jesus has puzzled the brightest minds in history. His wisdom has confounded great thinkers and philosophers. Ultimately, everyone who has studied the life and teachings of Jesus has been forced to accept Him—or reject His claim to be God in human flesh. Many have tried to find a middle ground, attempting to honor Him as a great human teacher while dismissing His claim to be the Son of God and the Savior of humanity. But as C. S. Lewis observed in *Mere Christianity*, that middle option is not available to us:

I am trying here to prevent anyone saying the

really foolish thing that people often say about Him: I'm ready to accept Jesus as a great moral teacher, but I don't accept his claim to be God. That is the one thing we must not say. A man who was merely a man and said the sort of things Jesus said would not be a great moral teacher. He would either be a lunatic—on the level with the man who says he is a poached egg—or else he would be the Devil of Hell. You must make your choice. Either this man was, and is, the Son of God, or else a madman or something worse. You can shut Him up for a fool, you can spit at Him and kill Him as a demon or you can fall at His feet and call Him Lord and God, but let us not come with any patronising nonsense about His being a great human teacher. He has not left that open to us. He did not intend to.[4]

We cannot simply accept Jesus as a great moral teacher while rejecting Him as Lord and Savior. We cannot be indifferent to Jesus. Many have tried, but Jesus has not left us that option. During His late-night conversation with Nicodemus, Jesus made it clear that neutrality is not an option: "For God did not send his Son into the world to condemn the world, but to save the world through him. Whoever believes in him is not condemned, but whoever does not believe stands condemned already because they have not believed in the name of God's one and only Son" (John 3:17-18).

If you try to remain neutral toward Jesus, if you choose to be indifferent toward Him, you are in the same category as those who reject Him. You may say, "But I consider myself a Christian. My parents are Christians. I'm a third-generation member of such-and-such denomination. Of course, I'm a Christian." That kind of "Christianity" won't save you. That's called "nominal Christianity"—being a "Christian" in name only. You are no better off as a "nominal Christian" than you are as a defiant atheist.

A gift of grace

We cannot earn God's indescribable gift. We cannot make ourselves worthy by our good works. It is a gift of God's grace, and we are utterly undeserving.

At Christmastime, we give gifts to each other—

but we cannot give as God gives. We give gifts to our friends and family members and colleagues. We give gifts to our children and grandchildren and nieces and nephews. Sometimes we give gifts to strangers we have compassion for, such as when we donate to the church food pantry or to the Salvation Army. Sometimes we give gifts to people who have a claim on us: "She gave me a gift last Christmas, so I guess I owe her a gift this Christmas."

But God does not give as we give. He gave this indescribable gift to humanity when humanity was at war with Him. He gave this gift to His enemies. Romans 5:8 tells us that, while we were still enemies of God, Christ died for us. In fact, God gave His greatest gift, the Christ of Christmas, to His enemies, not to His friends. He gave this gift knowing that humanity could not—would not—give Him anything in return.

Do you give gifts to enemies and antagonists, expecting nothing in return? Of course not. Only God gives this way. God in His grace gives the gift of Jesus to people who are undeserving and unworthy of that gift. He gave this gift to people who insulted Him and rebelled against Him.

People like me. People like you.

All genuine Christians have one thing in common: They are keenly aware that they are unworthy of the gift. That's why grace is defined as God's unmerited (that is, undeserved) favor. Grace is completely undeserved. We can't earn it. If you live 20,000 lifetimes, you will never be able to earn your way to heaven through good works.

So when God gave us His indescribable gift on that first Christmas, He did so *not* because we were good and had earned a reward for our goodness. Jesus did not come into the world to save good people, nice people, deserving people. The Bible tells us that Jesus came into the world to save sinners.

In the late 1960s, while the drug-drenched hippie movement was in full swing across America, another movement arose—the "Jesus People" movement. It began on the West Coast of America and quickly spread nationwide and around the world. It was an evangelical Christian revival that saved countless young lives from the drugs-and-sex lifestyle of the hippie counterculture.

In 1969, a song climbed the charts—a song

written to cash in on the "Jesus People" movement. It sold two million copies in its first year of release and lasted fourteen weeks on the Top 40 charts.[5] In the song, the singer claims he has never been a sinner, he's never sinned, and he has "a friend in Jesus." The song is a tragic parody of Christianity written by someone who knows nothing of the Christian gospel.

Please understand: As long as you think you're not a sinner, you are in serious danger of eternal death. In heaven, there will only be one person who never sinned, and that is Jesus the Lord. Everyone else in heaven will be a sinner saved by grace. Jesus came to save sinners.

The first step to receiving God's indescribable gift is to admit that you are a sinner. Jesus saves those who have come to the end of themselves, who know they are helpless to save themselves, who confess they have nothing to offer God. Jesus saves those who know they will never be good enough.

Do those words describe you? Then congratulations—you are now fully qualified to receive God's indescribable gift. That gift is reserved for those who have sinned and fall short of the glory of God.

Transforming power

God's indescribable gift produces amazing results in human lives.

It would take countless hours to tell you all the ways my life was transformed the moment Jesus came into my life. I was drifting aimlessly, without any goals for my life; Jesus gave my life focus and meaning. My family relationships were strained and dysfunctional; Jesus healed them. I had the wrong kind of friends who continually got me into trouble; Jesus gave me new friends who encouraged my walk with God.

How can you measure the impact of the forgiveness of all your sins—past, present, and future? God wipes the slate clean when you come to Him.

Consider the impact of this forgiveness on the life of the apostle Paul. He was a terrorist named Saul. He rounded up Christians and sent them to their death for the "crime" of being Christians. Then, as he was on the road to Damascus to take more Christians into custody, Jesus appeared to him and transformed his life. The indescribable gift turned Saul the terrorist into Paul the missionary.

That same indescribable gift even turned an ISIS terrorist leader into an evangelist for Jesus Christ. The 24/7 satellite TV ministry of *Leading The Way* is called THE KINGDOM SAT. It broadcasts the gospel across the Muslim world, from North Africa to the Philippines. Our field team member is named Peter.

One day, Peter received a call from a man we'll call Muhammad (not his real name) asking for an in-person meeting with Peter. Because of the danger of being ambushed by terrorists, our follow-up counselors never have in-person meetings until they have built a strong trust-relationship. Yet Peter sensed God saying to him, "Meet with this man. I have great plans for him." So Peter arranged a face-to-face meeting with Muhammad.

Peter didn't know at the time that Muhammad was a "prince of ISIS," a highly placed leader in the terror organization that called itself "the Islamic State." He held such a high rank in ISIS that others swore to obey his orders and even die for him. Muhammad was also a teacher of the

Qur'an.

"I had a strange feeling that he was from ISIS," Peter later recalled. "But I knew the Lord would protect me. God had a reason for this encounter, so even though I sensed danger, I was at peace."

Muhammad had been raised with a passion for leading Islam back to the era of militancy and conquest. One day, someone asked Muhammad why he followed Islam. How did he know it was true? Muhammad had no answer. He began searching the Qur'an, the Hadith, and the Sunnah for evidence that Allah exists and Islam is the truth—but he found none. He heard that a man named Peter talked to Muslims about Jesus, so he got Peter's phone number and called. He said nothing about being a prince of ISIS. He only said that he wanted to know the truth about God.

When the two men met, Peter sensed God urging him to speak boldly. He knew that Muslims thought that Allah in the Qur'an is identical to the God of the Bible. Peter began by bluntly smashing that idea. Looking the prince of ISIS squarely in the eye, he said, "Our God is not yours."

Muhammad was instantly enraged—and he considered killing Peter on the spot. He had a knife at the ready, tucked in his boot. But Peter went on to tell Muhammad about Jesus, who came to die as a sacrifice for our sins. Muhammad listened—and he began to cry. He didn't know why he was crying. It wasn't anything that Peter had said. He simply broke down—and he didn't reach for the knife.

Peter put his hand on Muhammad's shoulder and prayed for him. "As soon as I finished praying," Peter recalled, "he stood up and left me. I was relieved when he went away. I felt he was not stable. I felt that anything might happen."

For days afterward, Peter prayed for Muhammad, but heard no word from him. One day, Muhammad called and asked for another meeting. When Peter arrived, he saw that Muhammad seemed more troubled than ever. "I had a dream," the prince of ISIS said. "You were in my dream. You came to me and gave me a white envelope dripping with blood. The blood had a sweet fragrance, like perfume. When I saw the blood, I was scared. Then you said to me, 'Don't be afraid'—and I awoke from the dream. What does it mean?"

"The blood in the dream," Peter said, "is the blood of Jesus, that was shed for you. Without the shedding of blood, there is no forgiveness of sins."

Muhammad asked what he must do to be forgiven.

"The Lord has given you His forgiveness—for free. You just need to accept it."

That day, Peter began teaching and discipling Muhammad. They met frequently, prayed together, and studied God's Word together.

Finally, Muhammad confessed, "The first time I met with you, I had a knife and I intended to kill you. I'm sorry. I'm so sorry. In you, and in the Bible, I see a love that doesn't exist in Islam."

The former Prince of ISIS is now a follower of the Prince of Peace. A man of terror and war has found true peace. He has been baptized and now leads Bible studies. He even preaches the gospel to his old friends who were terrorists as well. "Jesus Christ is the truth," he said. "He is my life now."[6]

The indescribable gift of God transforms lives, with the power to transform even a prince of

ISIS into a Christian evangelist.

You might say, "Well, I'm not that bad. I could stand some improvement, but I've never killed anybody." My friend, it makes no difference whether you miss His standard of righteousness by two inches or two miles. If you miss the mark at all, you are a sinner. Only Jesus, God's indescribable gift, can take your sin away and bring you eternal life.

When I received God's indescribable gift, I knew my sins were forgiven and God had erased my sin and guilt. The Bible tells us that God throws our sins into the depths of the deepest sea, that He removes our sins as far as the east is from the west. Not only does God remove our sin, but He replaces it with an indescribable peace and joy, even in our darkest days.

Our "heavenly Daddy"

God's indescribable gift also grants us adoption status. We become full-fledged children of God—and God becomes our "heavenly Daddy." Before receiving God's indescribable gift, you were a stranger from God. You were separated from God. You were excluded from heaven. But

God's indescribable gift entitles you to be called a son or daughter of God. You are not a slave. You are not a servant. You are a child and an heir of the living God. You will inherit the estate of your heavenly Daddy.

Does it seem strange to hear God referred to as "Daddy"? Yet this concept comes straight from God's Word. In Mark 14:36, Jesus agonizes in the Garden of Gethsemane and He prays, "Abba, Father, everything is possible for you. Take this cup from me. Yet not what I will, but what you will." In Aramaic, the word "Abba" is a child's name for his or her father—the equivalent of "Daddy."

And the apostle Paul tells us that, when we accepted the gift of salvation, we received the Holy Spirit, who has sealed our adoption as God's children. We read this in Romans 8:15, where Paul writes, "The Spirit you received does not make you slaves, so that you live in fear again; rather, the Spirit you received brought about your adoption to sonship. And by him we cry, 'Abba, Father.'" And in Galatians 4:6, Paul writes, "Because you are his sons, God sent the Spirit of his Son into our hearts, the Spirit who calls out, 'Abba, Father.'"

God is not a stern and remote Father. Our God is Abba, Daddy, the Father who lifts us up and puts us on His knee and delights in us. He is our loving heavenly Daddy, and we are His children and heirs. Normally you inherit an estate after a parent dies. But we inherit God's estate when *we* die, because our heavenly Father *never* dies. But we cannot inherit heaven unless we receive God's indescribable gift.

Today, we hear many voices in society saying that God receives everybody when they die. Everyone goes to heaven, they say. But you won't find this teaching in the Bible. It is a lie straight from the pit of hell, intended to mislead people into squandering their lives and their eternal souls. It's sad and tragic that so many people have believed this lie. I have known such people—and I have wept tears of sorrow at their gravesides.

But you and I can say, with the apostle Paul in 2 Corinthians 9:15, "Thanks be to God for his indescribable gift!"

I have had the privilege of circling the globe dozens of times throughout my years of ministry. I have set foot on every continent except Antarctica. I have spoken with countless people who have received God's indescribable gift. And I have never met a single person who said, "I received this gift, but I wish I hadn't. I regret having wasted so many years following Christ." I haven't met anyone who feels that receiving Christ as Lord and Savior was a mistake.

Of course, I've met many Christians who said, "If only I had accepted Christ earlier in life! If only I had made Jesus the Lord of my life when I was younger! Why did I wait so long? Why did I waste so many years living for myself?"

You may be a young person with your whole life ahead of you—or you may be an elderly person with most of your life in the rearview mirror. That doesn't matter. All that matters is that, today, when you hear His voice, don't delay. Don't harden your heart. Don't reject the gift of true peace.

Receive God's indescribable gift, right here, right now.

7

The Only Response

The late pastor and conference speaker Jerry Cook told a story of a young drug dealer. This young man was in his apartment, using illegal drugs with his girlfriend, when he turned to her and said he would give anything to be free of his drug addiction.

"I know how you can do that," she replied.

"How?"

"If you trusted in Jesus as your Savior, He would deliver you."

The young man was intrigued. He questioned her further and learned that she had been raised in a Christian home and her parents had taught her the Bible throughout her childhood. In her rebellion, she had resisted committing her life to Jesus Christ. The young man asked her what it meant to trust in Jesus as his Savior.

She said, "I'm not going to tell you."

"Why not?"

"Because then you'll take off and be a Christian and I won't see you anymore."

But the young man was tired of his meaningless life. He pleaded with her to tell him how to find true peace and freedom from his addiction.

Finally, she said, "All right, I'll tell you." Though she was not a Christian and wanted nothing to do with Jesus, she explained God's plan of salvation to him. She quoted the words of Jesus in John 3:16: "For God so loved the world that he gave his one and only Son, that whoever believes in him shall not perish but have eternal life." Then she explained that he should pray, admit that he was a sinner, and ask Jesus to take control of his life.

The young man got up, went into another room, and asked Jesus to come and take over his life. Then he got up, said goodbye to his girlfriend, and walked out of the apartment. He never came back and he never used drugs again. From that day forward, he lived for Christ.

And what happened to his girlfriend? As far as Jerry Cook knew, she never gave her life to Jesus Christ. Though she acknowledged that Jesus alone had the power to save, though she had reluctantly led her boyfriend to Christ, she herself wanted nothing to do with Jesus.[7]

The Christian gospel is so simple and powerful that even a rebellious and unwilling person can share the life-changing good news. Jesus truly is the way, the truth, and the life. No one comes to the Father except through Him. When you hear that story, there is only one response that leads to true peace and eternal life.

Any other response ends in death.

Invited into a relationship

It's important to take time out from the pressures of this life to think seriously about the end of life and the life *beyond* this life. From time to time, we need to ask ourselves, "What am I living for? What place does God have in my life? What will happen to me when I die?"

Most of us avoid such questions throughout

our lives. We think there's plenty of time to think about such things. We think our lives will go on and on forever, and we can keep putting off questions of life and death.

"I'm just not a religious person," you might say. "I've been in churches before, and they're full of hypocrites. I want nothing to do with religion."

The Lord Jesus would be the first to agree that there are hypocrites in the religious world. When He preached in ancient Palestine, He was repeatedly attacked by self-important religious leaders—and Jesus called them hypocrites to their faces. These same people plotted to crucify Him.

But God is not recruiting you to a *religion*. He's inviting you into a *relationship*.

When Adam and Eve were created, they didn't have a religion. They didn't need a religion. They had a *relationship* with God. They were on intimate terms with Him, and He was their friend. And that's exactly the relationship God wants to have with you.

All He asks is that you place your trust in the saving power of His Son Jesus, that you turn away from your sins and surrender your life to

Him. Once you sincerely commit your life to Him, He will begin to transform your life and your character. You'll set out on a lifelong journey with the Lord Jesus.

Does that mean you'll never be tempted again? No. Only Jesus was without sin. You will experience temptation—but you won't face it alone. God will send His Holy Spirit to live in you. Your life will demonstrate increasing evidence of the qualities the Bible calls "the fruit of the Spirit"—qualities of love, joy, peace, patience, kindness, goodness, faithfulness, gentleness, and self-control.

God sends His Holy Spirit to every genuine believer. The Spirit will empower you to live for Him and seal your permanent adoption as a child of God. As the Spirit gains more and more control of your life, He will reshape and redirect your life. He will confirm your true identity as a child of the living God.

When your earthly life is over, you'll go home to be with your Father in heaven. There, you'll experience life as it was meant to be lived when God placed Adam and Eve in the Garden of Eden. In heaven, there will be no crime, no corruption. You'll experience no suffering, no sickness, no sorrow. Death and pain will be no more—so, of course, there will be no more tears. It will be a place of true peace and joy.

Heaven will also be a realm of adventure. God will give us work to do in heaven—exciting, meaningful service. Just as God gave Adam and Eve enjoyable work to do in the Garden of Eden, He will give us responsibilities to carry out in eternity. The book of Revelation tells us that God's people will serve Him in heaven throughout eternity (Revelation 22:3). Imagine—there will not be one millisecond of boredom in heaven.

Yes, we will rest from our spiritual struggles. We will be free from guilt and regret. Yes, we will experience an eternity of true peace. But we will also be very busy serving Jesus as we reign forever with Him.

This world is impermanent and destined for destruction. But if we have placed our trust in Him, then we are citizens of the world to come—a permanent world called heaven.

No finer way to live—and die

The imperishable reality of heaven is what every heart longs for. We all want a home where we can live forever, experience endless joy in God's presence, and be reunited with those we love. God Himself placed those desires within us, so that we would never be satisfied with anything less than eternity with Him. He wants to draw us into a relationship with Him, because only by joining our lives to His can we experience the eternal life He intended for us at creation.

God made us in His image so that we would reflect His mind and His heart. He created us to experience friendship with Him. We are physical beings—but we are not *merely* physical. We are part of the spiritual realm, and we were created for heaven. We are dissatisfied with life until we find our true destiny with Him. Only when our searching leads us home to the Father can we find the true peace and belonging we seek.

As the Bible tells us, God has "set eternity in the hearts of men" (Ecclesiastes 3:11). You and I were made for heaven. In his book *Heaven*, Randy Alcorn writes, "We are homesick for Eden. We are nostalgic for what is implanted in our hearts. It's built into us, perhaps even at a genetic level. We long for what the first man and woman once enjoyed—a perfect and beautiful Earth with free and untainted relationships with God, each other, animals, and our environment. Every attempt at human progress has been an attempt to overcome what was lost in the Fall."[8]

Down through history, God has sometimes allowed His followers to see a glimpse of heaven while they were still alive on earth. In the New Testament, we read the story of Stephen, who was stoned to death as the first Christian martyr. The account tells us that, as the enraged mob picked up stones and closed in around him, "Stephen, full of the Holy Spirit, looked up to heaven and saw the glory of God, and Jesus standing at the right hand of God. 'Look,' he said, 'I see heaven open and the Son of Man standing at the right hand of God'" (Acts 7:55-56). As Stephen said this, the people rushed at him and stoned him to death.

Another believer who was granted a glimpse of heaven before he died was evangelist Dwight L. Moody (1837-1899). On November 16, 1899, Moody preached a sermon at a church in Kansas City, Kansas. Afterwards, he collapsed. Though the doctors didn't know the cause of his illness, Moody suffered from congestive heart failure.

Sensing death approaching, Moody confided to his closest friends, "Soon you will read in the newspaper that I am dead. Don't believe it for a moment. I will be more alive than ever before."

Three days before Christmas, Moody lay on his deathbed. His family and friends gathered around him to say goodbye. Though he struggled to breathe, Moody had no fear of death. His eyes were alight with peace and joy. Those who were with him said that he seemed to see things no one else could see. His last words were, "Earth recedes . . . Heaven opens before me!"

Then he passed into the presence of his Lord.

There is no finer way to live—and no better way to die—than to live and die as a follower of Christ. It's an incredible blessing to know your sins are forgiven, to know you have a right relationship with God, and to know He has welcomed you with open arms, just as the loving father welcomed the prodigal son.

Tomorrow may be too late

After Adam and Eve sinned, God promised a Deliverer who would save the people from their sins. Some 2,000 years ago, at God's appointed time, He fulfilled all of the prophecies through His Son, Jesus Christ. The Lord Jesus paid the price and endured the punishment for our sins— for the sins of everyone who comes to Him and receives Him. That is God's plan of salvation for you and me.

A day is coming when Jesus will sit on the judgment bench. The human race will come before Him to be judged. There will be those who accepted God's gracious gift—and those who chose their own way. Jesus will send away those who tried to water down or rewrite His plan according to their own self-centered desires.

You must ask yourself: Am I willing to accept God's gift of eternal life? Am I willing to take Jesus at His word when He says, "I am the way and the truth and the life. No one comes to the Father except through me"? Your eternal life depends on your answer to this question.

Some claim that it's narrow-minded and intolerant to say there's only one path to God. But Jesus said, "Enter through the narrow gate. For wide is the gate and broad is the road that leads to destruction, and many enter through it. But small is the gate and narrow the road that leads to life, and only a few find it" (Matthew 7:13-14).

If you want to enter Walt Disney World or board an airliner, you have to pass through a narrow gate. You can't climb over a wall or slip through a back door or come up through a trap door. You can only enter through the narrow gate.

The gate that leads to God may be narrow, but it's clearly marked. God has told you how to be saved. His requirements are not burdensome. You do not have to crawl on your knees over broken glass. You do not have to memorize any passwords. You do not have to cover yourself with sackcloth and ashes. You simply come to Jesus and ask Him to be Lord of your life.

Your loving Father in heaven invites you to have fellowship with Him. Now you must respond. There are only two possible responses to His invitation: Accept it or reject it. Believe in Jesus and follow the narrow path—or turn your back on Him and go your own way.

You can say to God, "No, thanks. I like the broad path. I like to think that there are many ways to heaven. I don't like the narrow way. Like Adam and Eve, like the prodigal son, I'm going to go my own way."

God has told you clearly what lies at the end of such a decision: Destruction. Adam and Eve made that decision and were exiled from the garden. The prodigal son made that same decision and ended up alone and destitute in a far country.

You may say, "I can reject God now and come back to Him later. I can go my own way for a while. I can party now and come back to Him, just as the prodigal son returned to his father."

Perhaps. But you are taking a terrible risk with your eternal destiny. You never know how much time you have on this earth. Today could be the last day of your life. You may never get another chance to make this decision. Right now, God is speaking to you and urging you to accept the free gift He offers you. This may be the closest you'll ever come to making that decision. Tomorrow may be too late.

So I urge you to make a choice before another moment slips by: Eternal life in heaven in the presence of God—or torment in hell where Satan dwells. I don't make the rules. You don't make the rules. God makes the rules. He says there is only one way—a narrow way—and the name of that way is Jesus.

The moment of decision

A husband and wife came to me for counseling because the young woman was wracked with guilt over a sin she had committed years earlier. I told her that, if she had confessed her sin and received Jesus as her Lord and Savior, then God had forgiven and erased her sins. But she could not accept that. She sobbed uncontrollably, saying, "I can't believe that God would forgive all my sins. It's too good to be true. My sins are too awful to forgive."

I said, "Let me tell you a story. Caesar Augustus, the Emperor of Rome, once gave a friend an incredibly expensive gift. His friend refused it, saying, 'I cannot accept such a gift. It is too much for me to receive!' Augustus replied, 'Yes, but it's not too much for me to give.' God's forgiveness is like that gift. Such a gift may be hard for you to receive—but Jesus was not too much for God to give. He wants to give you this gift. Don't refuse it. Don't say it's too good to be true. Just accept Jesus and thank Him for the gift of eternal life."

So she prayed and thanked God—and she

received the blessing of complete forgiveness.

It's time for *you* to make a decision. Will you accept Him now? Your loving Father in heaven is ready and eager to accept you. Here is a prayer of decision and commitment you can pray:

Dear heavenly Father,

Thank You for Your love for me, a sinner. I know that I have violated Your moral law many times throughout my life. But Lord, I'm sorry and I want to turn away from my sin and live for You. I invite Jesus to come into my life as Lord and Savior, to take control of my life from this day forward. Father, forgive my sin and receive me as Your child.

Thank You for hearing my prayer and receiving me. Please seal this decision I've made and help me live the rest of my life for You. Live Your life through me. Guide me as I read Your Word.

Thank You in Jesus' name. Amen.

If you prayed those words honestly and sincerely, then you have begun a new life with Jesus Christ. You are a child of the King, a member of His royal family.

Take note of this date. In the days and years to come, the decision you have just made will become more and more meaningful. Pray daily. Read God's Word. Seek regular fellowship with other Christians. Attend a church where you can grow in your faith and be baptized. Take part in a mid-week Bible study. As you take these steps, you'll grow stronger and deeper in your faith. Your friendship and fellowship with God will become more and more real to you.

As you grow in your Christian life, you'll discover an ever-deeper love for God (see Matthew 10:37) and a growing desire to spend time with Him in prayer (see Luke 18:1; Ephesians 6:18). You'll discover the joy of getting to know other Christians and praying with them (see Acts 2:42; 1 John 4:7-8). And you'll grow in your obedience to God (see John 14:15; 15:10).

Throughout your life, you'll know the true peace that only comes from a relationship with Jesus Christ. As Jesus Himself said, "Peace I leave with you; my peace I give you. I do not give to you as the world gives. Do not let your hearts be troubled and do not be afraid" (John 14:27). God's

Word promises that a relationship with Jesus brings us "the peace of God, which transcends all understanding"—a peace that guards our hearts and minds in Him (Philippians 4:7).

Thank God every day for this gift of salvation He has given you. And don't keep it to yourself—tell everyone around you what God has done for you. And please write to me and tell me about your decision to follow Jesus Christ.

God bless you as you live for Him!

Dr. Michael Youssef
Leading The Way
PO Box 20100
Atlanta, Georgia, USA 30325
Or call: 833-KNOW-HIM (833-566-9446)

For more information about
Leading The Way and its mission to passionately proclaim uncompromising Truth around the world, visit LTW.org today.

Notes

[1] Deepak Chopra, *The Third Jesus: The Christ We Cannot Ignore* (New York: Random House, 2008), pp. 9-10.

[2] Russell H. Conwell, *Acres of Diamonds* (Philadelphia: Temple University Press, 2002), pp. 2-12.

[3] Richard Crashaw, "A Hymn of the Nativity" (public domain), collected by Henry Charles Beeching, ed., *Lyra Sacra: A Book of Religious Verse* (1903), Bartleby.com, https://www.bartleby.com/296/97.html.

[4] C. S. Lewis, *Mere Christianity* (New York, NY: Touchstone, 1996), p. 56.

[5] Tom McNichol, "A 'Spirit' From the '60s That Won't Die," *New York Times*, December 24, 2006, https://www.nytimes.com/2006/12/24/fashion/24norman.html.

[6] Michael Youssef, *The Hidden Enemy: Aggressive Secularism, Radical Islam, and the Fight for Our Future* (Carol Stream, IL: Tyndale, 2018), pp. 196-198.

[7] Jerry Cook with Stanley C. Baldwin, *Love, Acceptance and Forgiveness: Equipping the Church to Be Truly Christian in a Non-Christian World* (Ventura, CA: Regal Books, 1979), pp. 69-70.

[8] Randy Alcorn, *Heaven* (Wheaton, Illinois: Tyndale, 2004), p. 77.

Are you...

▶ Searching for answers?
▶ In need of prayer?
▶ Ready to give your life to Christ?

Speak to our team of pastors today at:
FindingTruePeace.com

Discover More
from Michael Youssef and
Leading The Way

DOWNLOAD THE FREE APP TODAY

 Inspiring Messages

 Daily Devotionals

 Bible Reading Plan

AVAILABLE NOW:

Keyword: *Leading The Way*